# CAKE WRECKS

# CAKE WRECKS

## When Professional Cakes Go Hilariously Wrong

Jen Yates

**Andrews McMeel
Publishing, LLC**

Kansas City · Sydney · London

ISBN-13: 978-0-7407-8537-5
ISBN-10: 0-7407-8537-0

Library of Congress Control Number: 2009925842

09 10 11 12 13 TWP 10 9 8 7 6 5 4 3

Book design by Holly Camerlinck

www.andrewsmcmeel.com

Attention: Schools and Businesses

Andrews McMeel books are available at quantity discounts with bulk purchase for educational, business, or sales promotional use. For information, please write to: Special Sales Department, Andrews McMeel Publishing, LLC, 1130 Walnut Street, Kansas City, Missouri 64106.

For the fans of CakeWrecks.com.

Wreckies, Wrecktators, or
Evil Wrecky Henchpersons—
by any name, y'all rock.

# Contents

# Acknowledgments

Cake Wrecks has been nothing short of a miracle in my life, so I have to first thank God for the amazing whirlwind of a journey this past year and a half has been. It hasn't always been easy, but I wouldn't trade my life now for anything or anyone's.

I'm also deeply indebted to Christopher Schelling, my agent extraordinaire; my amazing editor Chris Schillig, Holly Camerlinck, and the entire team at Andrews McMeel; my "Wrecksistant" Anne-Marie; and my go-to genius Chris Friend. Thanks also to Marian Lizzi, Mom and Dad, Mum, my big brother Ben, and the amazing network of friends who have either held my hand or kicked my butt as needed throughout this process. John and Abby, Josh and Alison, Julianne, and Heather, you guys get the gold stars.

And finally, none of this would have been possible without my husband, John. From carrying me through the hard times to laughing with me through the good ones, he shows me daily what love looks like. He also does a mean Swedish Chef

impersonation and likes to bake—but not eat—
brownies. If that's not the whole package, then I
don't know what is. Thanks, sweetie—I love you.

# The Cake That Started It All:

## A Brief History of Cake Wrecks

In May 2008, a few days after my thirtieth birthday, I got an e-mail that made me laugh. You've probably seen it; it was one of those viral funnies that got forwarded about a billion times, and probably is still making the rounds. Heck, I bet right now someone in Bangladesh is chortling while forwarding this thing on to everyone in her address book. Anyway, on the off chance you *haven't* seen it, the photo in the e-mail looked something like this:

It's not hard to imagine the phone order that led to this cake. What *is* hard to imagine is how someone could transcribe the order so literally and yet manage to misspell it at the same time. Is there something profound at work here? Some great social commentary on the mind-numbing qualities of low-paying, repetitious work?

Or are people just dumb sometimes?

Whatever the reason, it's funny stuff. Nothing monumental, of course, but a good gag to chuckle over before moving on to that business proposition from the prince of Nigeria.

And yet, as I looked at it that day, a little light-bulb went on. Then I got an idea. I already had some other funny cake photos saved from my searches for inspirational designs for my cake-decorating class. So I started thinking, what if I posted these online somewhere? What would I say? The answers made me chuckle. (Sure, I laugh at my own jokes. Doesn't everyone?)

"Hey, what do you think of the name 'Cake Wrecks'?" I called to my husband. "You know, like 'train wreck,' only with 'cake'?"

"I like it," he said, popping his head into my office. "Why? Are you going to put those on a blog?"

"Yeah, I think so. You know, just for fun."

And just like that, Cake Wrecks was born.

I waited about a week before I told anyone about it. By then scouring the Net for more pictures each night was my new hobby. It was fun; I relished the hunt, and I *loved* snarking on what I found. Posting everything anonymously made it all the sweeter, because it gave my rather wicked sense of humor free rein. (I'm actually painfully polite in person—ask anybody.) When I did e-mail a few friends the site address, I kept it pretty low-key. (In fact, when my mother-in-law first started reading the site, she had no idea I was the author.) I wasn't out to attract readers, and I certainly knew nothing about professional blogging: This was purely something for my own amusement.

After posting for several weeks, I was shocked one night to find a comment on the site from *someone I didn't know*. Even though it was very complimentary, initially I was actually a bit consternated. People I didn't know were reading my blog! But as more comments started trickling in over the next few weeks, I realized these people I didn't know actually *liked* it. I was thrilled, and suddenly the thought of strangers reading my blog didn't bother me nearly as much.

The weekend of July 4 someone posted a link to Cake Wrecks on the message board of a large cake community Web site. Traffic shot up: I'm talking like two hundred people a day, peeps! I'd hit the big time! Even better, people started e-mailing me photos. I had thought there wasn't enough material out there to keep Cake Wrecks afloat for more than a few months. My faithful Wreckporters, as I came to call them, proved me wrong and saved the site from an early demise.

The next month saw some huge spikes in readership thanks to links from a few other major Web sites, and the site traffic continued to grow by staggering leaps and bounds. By this time I was using my first name on posts, since being completely anonymous was confusing for readers, and soon I was getting requests for interviews and even some media coverage. "Flabbergasted" is the best word to describe my reaction over the next few months. Considering I never advertised the site in any way, its growth and success were really nothing short of astounding. By February '09, over fifty thousand people from around the globe were reading Cake Wrecks every day, with hundreds of e-mails arriving each month.

So what is it about messed-up cakes that people find so appealing? I can't say for sure, but I think it has something to do with the fact that almost all of us have a cake story to tell. Maybe it was that Barbie or He-Man cake you were so thrilled with on your seventh birthday, or the ridiculous homemade heap your roommate made to cheer you up after so-and-so dumped you, or your oh-so-perfect wedding cake—the one Uncle Jerry knocked over at the reception during his drunken rendition of the "Thriller" dance. Good or bad, these cakes tell little stories about us. So when we see a cake with the inscription "Sorry for all those things we said" or one that's shaped like a toilet plunger, we know there's probably a story behind *it*, too—and if we're lucky, a really funny one. Whether we get that story or are left having to imagine it, these little slices of flawed humanity can make us feel more connected to each other. Hey, everyone's a little stupid sometimes, right? And we've all made mistakes. Cake Wrecks remind us to never take ourselves too seriously, and that nothing in life is a total loss if it makes you smile.

## Why Buy the Cow?: Book vs. Blog

If you're already familiar with Cake Wrecks, you'll be happy to know that this book is more than just the blog put to paper. Here you'll learn a bit more about me, the Wrecks, the people who make the Wrecks, the people who *find* the Wrecks, and some of the best "cake disaster" stories out there. I'll also fill you in on the crazy controversies you never knew cake could create, the "fun" side to

Internet trolls, and how Wreckporters are terrorizing local bakeries. I'll even answer the question "what was she *thinking*?" for some of the most (and least) popular Wrecks. And don't worry; there will also be lots (and lots) of new, never-before-seen Wreckage. I wouldn't leave out the feature presentation, now, would I?

# What's a Wreck? Some Helpful "Guidelines"

Obviously when you label something a Cake Wreck it helps if folks know what that means. So here's my working definition:

## "A CAKE WRECK IS ANY PROFESSIONALLY MADE CAKE THAT IS UNINTENTIONALLY SAD, SILLY, CREEPY, INAPPROPRIATE—YOU NAME IT. *A WRECK IS NOT NECESSARILY A POORLY MADE CAKE;* IT'S SIMPLY ONE I FIND FUNNY, FOR ANY NUMBER OF REASONS."

Thats right, folks, *I* make the call. Me! [rubbing hands together in fiendish delight] And if you don't like it, tough cookies! *Mwu-ha-ha-haaa!*

Er, what I *mean* to say is: If you don't agree that something in this book is a Wreck, then just remember that *some* Wrecks are a matter of opinion. (And mine is the only opinion that counts here. So *there*.) Also remember that Cake Wrecks are like car wrecks: They're not always the fault of the driver/decorator. After all, sometimes a boozed-up idiot runs a red light, or demands a cake that looks like a giant fungus-riddled foot. In those cases, sure, the baker may have perfectly sculpted the oozing toenails, but guess what? It's still a Wreck in my book. (Oh, and hey . . . it *is* my book! Suh-weet!)

The next thing people ask is what I mean by "professionally made." The easy answer is "any cake that someone was paid to create." However, that's not entirely accurate; obviously if you paid your Aunt Edna to "give it a go" on your wedding cake, well first, you're an idiot, but second, I won't call it a Wreck. Why? Because that'd be too easy, and I'm not one to settle for cheap shots. (Unless they're *really* funny, that is.) So I check sources, question the submitter, and basically do

everything in my power to ensure your Aunt Edna's little experiment doesn't end up labeled an official Wreck. As such, you can rest assured that everything in this book (unless listed otherwise) really was professionally created. You may have to keep reminding yourself of that as you go.

## The Disclaimer

I am not the consumer watchdog of cakes. I'm not out to shame cake decorators or hurt bakery sales. In fact, nothing in this book should be taken too seriously. I created Cake Wrecks to find the funny in unexpected, sugar-filled places. If I've managed to make some folks laugh along the way, well heck, that's just the icing on the . . . aw, *you* know.

## A Word on Photo Quality

All of the pictures in this book were taken and submitted by readers of CakeWrecks.com. They are not "artistic," "properly lit," or necessarily "in focus." Most were taken on the front lines: in the bakeries themselves. Valiant Wreckporters the world over have risked their reputations, well-being, and continued shopping pleasure to bring us this documentation. They braved looks-to-kill from bakers, puzzled glances from fellow customers, and even the occasional managerial request to vacate the premises. Let us then applaud these heroic souls and enjoy their bounty in the spirit in which it was offered: with humility, appreciation, and minimal whining about window glare.

Oh, and you'll notice that the bakery labels in the photos have all been removed. There is a very simple yet compelling reason for this: I hate lawsuits.

Now, on to the Wreckage!

# Literal LOLs

Some Wrecks make you wonder what exactly the customer ordered. Not these!

*"King of Fire logo here"*

"What would you like on the cake?"

"Nothing."

When the "Lady in Red" procreates, perhaps?

## I'm With "Ulations"

Tammy writes:

"When I graduated from high school my mom ordered a cake that said 'Congratulations Tammy!' Pretty simple, you'd think, but a wrench was thrown into the baker's plans when my mom later called to say that we'd be needing more cake (there were more RSVPs than she expected).

"The big day came, and we picked up two cakes from the bakery. The first cake read:

"Congrat
Tam"

And as you might have guessed, the second cake read:

"ulations
my!"

Tammy tells me that to this day, "Ulations my!" is still how her family congratulates each other.

When in doubt, "add quotation marks" (and parentheses, for good measure).

Sorry, you can't have any.

Boy, Cole & Alli are NOT going to be happy about this.

"What, we're not good enough for the large font? Huh? HUH?"

So Dawn was throwing a *Wizard of Oz* cast party, and being a veteran Cake Wrecks reader she knew better than to order anything complicated. Instead, she simply asked for a cake with "Somewhere Over the Rainbow" on it.

Now, given the examples you've seen so far, you would be forgiven for thinking that the resulting cake would look like this:

"Some Wear"
The Rainbow

I'm pleased to report that's not what happened, however. No, Dawn received something far more . . . colorful.

At first I thought the decorator was just being clever, but then I noticed the "Somewheres." Hm. Well, there went *that* theory.

Here's a tip: If your message is "Phillip . . . Woo-hoo!" and you actually have to *say* the words "dot dot dot," be prepared for just about anything.

We can't forget the cake that started it all:

"Best Wishes Suzanne
Under Neat that
We will Miss you."

"And underneath that, write 'We will miss you.' Got it?"

Oh yeah, they got it.

As I mentioned in "The Cake That Started It All," this cake really got around the forwarded e-mail circuit in 2008. For a period of four or five months there, I was getting it submitted about a dozen times a week. I was forced to add a submission "guidelines" page, mostly to tell everyone to stop sending me the "underneat that" cake! Even then, people *still* sent it in. Truly, this must be the world's most famous Cake Wreck. Its origins are pretty mundane, though: According to a reader who worked with the famous Suzanne, this was the office send-off cake when she switched jobs.

# The Dreaded CCC

Cake Wrecks come in many forms, but there is one form that has proven itself to be particularly insidious in the world of baked goods. Where for most cakey creations the Wreck is the exception, in this guise it proves to be the rule. I'm talking, of course, about the cupcake cake—or CCC for short.

As the name suggests, a CCC is a cake (or "cake") made up of cupcakes. Innocent-seeming in theory, this construct of unspeakable proportions, flawed breeding, and misguided conception has entranced the U.S. population with its promises of "less mess," "equal portions," and "fun for all ages!" and now has begun creeping inexorably onward to other countries. It is a roving terror, bent on the destruction of decency, clean fingers, and proper cake-to-icing ratio.

What, you don't believe me? Ah, then perhaps you are one of the blissfully uninitiated in these culinary catastrophes! Allow me to walk you through the unholy assemblage of a CCC.

## Step 1:

Glue cupcakes (in their paper wrappers) to a board using icing. Lots of icing.

## Step 2:

Slop on a layer of icing approximately 1.5–2 inches in thickness, smoothing over the gaps between cupcakes like drywall mud over, er . . . drywall. (See reference photo, left.)

 **This is the proper icing-to-cupcake ratio for a CCC.**

## Step 3:

"Decorate."

When done, you end up with something like you see on the next page.

# Yummy.

My readers tell me this says "Ojai, 'It's worth the drive!'" but let's ignore the random quotation marking for the moment and instead focus on all that baked poo soufflé goodness, shall we?

I mean, it takes an uncommon skill to achieve that kind of texture. In fact, this CCC visually sums up my feelings on cupcake cakes in general, but of course I know you're going to want more examples. (Picky, picky!)

Generally speaking, CCCs fall into one of three categories, depending on the baker's personality.

First, there's the **Steamrolled CCC,** characterized by its lumpy edges and general "run over by a cement truck" appearance:

This type of CCC is less malevolent and more misguided. Its limping sadness speaks of squashed frustration and defeat. The decorator didn't *intend* for it to be this ugly: He or she just couldn't help it.

(What the cement truck driver saw after backing up, perhaps?)

Here's another example, and a fan favorite over on CakeWrecks.com.

Now, you may be thinking this is actually a pretty good representation of Teen Wolf, had he met an untimely demise by way of a falling piano. However, what the customer *ordered* was Curious George—you know, the cute little monkey? Yeeeaah.

Next is the **Lazy and/or Stingy Decorator's CCC.** Some bakeries recognize that no one wants the mess of the more traditional—i.e., spackled together—CCC, while others recognize that using five pounds of frosting per CCC costs more than using only two pounds of frosting. So to compromise (and save money), these bakeries place individually iced cupcakes together and then decorate them as a whole, like so:

A half-rotten apple?

Nope, a guitar! (Duh!)

These CCCs result in what large chain bakeries call a "win-win". The CCC's intended design is now completely unrecognizable, and they're saving money on frosting. (They do, however, make sure there's still enough icing around the bottom edges of the wrappers to ensure no one will escape with clean hands. Rules are rules.)

Apparently Wall-E has gone to the dark side, and is advancing on rebel worlds in his very own imperial cruiser.

Plus, the invention of large plastic "decor kits" allows even the most
palsy-stricken in the blind community to join the fun:

It's like the Shake 'n Bake of decorating: just add cupcakes and various
plastic appendages, secure the lid, and then have a little fit on the way to the display rack.
Guaranteed to be more fun than a barrel of monkey limbs!

Next is what I've affectionately titled the **"WTF" CCC.** This is for all those passive-aggressive bakers out there. It says, "I value this job only as far as my next paycheck, and confounding customers with my inept and nonsensical creations is the best perk I get this side of free day-old doughnuts." Sure, we customers get the short end of the stick, but it's nice to know these civil servants have found a nonviolent outlet for their frustrations.

Some examples:

A candy-cane-shaped wreath. With a face. [nodding slowly] Ohhh-kay. Sure, no, I see where you're going with this. And if I'm not mistaken, they have some spiffy padded rooms there.

Rattles? Balloons? Those bouncy things you sit on? Or simply a compelling case for more art funding in public schools?

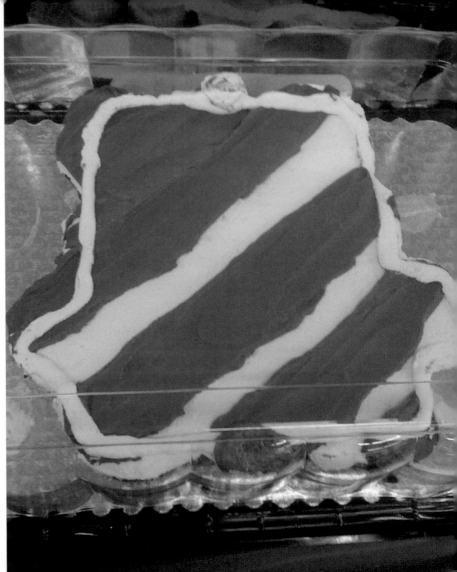

I have no idea. None.

"Footprints on your heart?" You mean, that's supposed to be a *foot*? Dang, girl, I think you'd better lay off the YogaToes.

And as with many Wrecks, I'm forced to wonder just what kind of occasion calls for this sort of cake. Consoling a dumpee, perhaps? One who has metaphorical footprints all over his or her metaphorical heart after it was metaphorically stomped on?

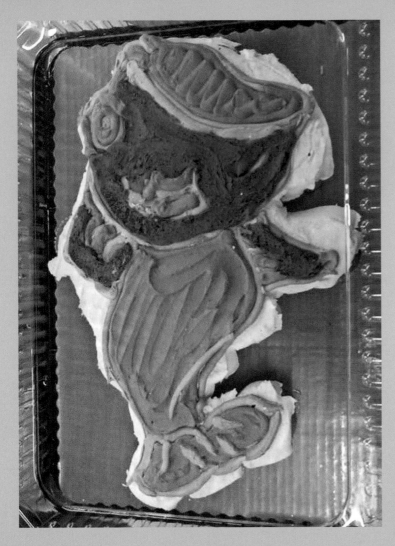

I don't know what this is,
but I swear it's giving me
the stink-eye.

When asked to explain these creations,
decorators will often respond with a carefully
practiced "huh?" apathetic shrug, or "I dunno;
that was [insert other employee's name]'s job."
It's foolproof: No one can pierce their ironclad
defenses.

# YOUR TURN!

See if you can ID a few of these CCCs:

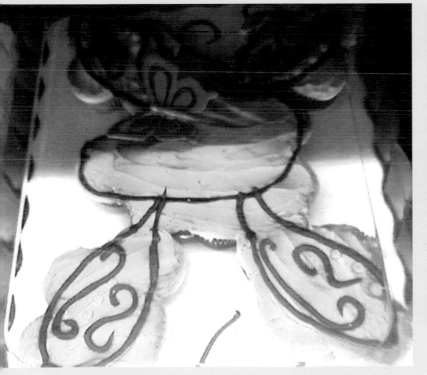

Butterfly, my foot: I know a diagram of a frog autopsy when I see one.

Part of me is curious what it would be like to live in a world where this design makes sense. The other part wants more sprinkles.

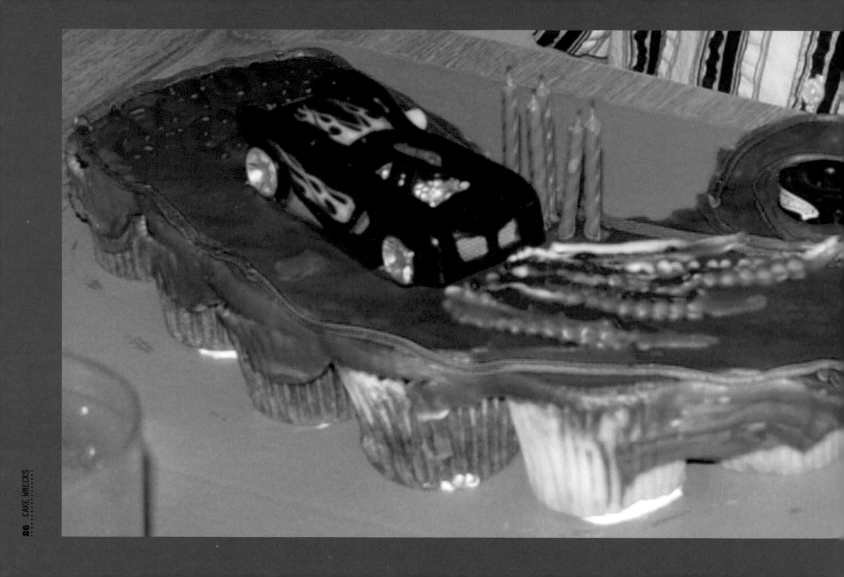

# "WHAT'S THAT YOU SAY? SORRY, I CAN'T HEAR YOU OVER THIS WRECK"

[squinting] From what I can see, this appears to be a pimpmobile leaving behind a trail of crinkle-cut French fries in a radioactive river of blood—only it's a radioactive river of blood with jaunty blue outlining.

I love the extra cupcake stuck on the side, too. What's that supposed to be a pit stop?

If you want to give yourself a migraine, try reading what it says in front of the car. Don't see any writing? Look closer. No, closer. (Pay no mind to that popping sound; it's just your eye capillaries going.)

Well, I've made my point the best way I know how: with sweeping generalizations. (And before you send me letters—yes, I *do* realize that there is the occasional "good" CCC—kind of like there is the occasional twelve-toed cat.) It's my fervent hope that you will join with me and your fellow baked-goods lovers in just saying no to CCCs, so that in time these wrecktastic creations will be relegated to the "what were we thinking?" past, alongside mullets, low-carb diets, and pretty much the entire decade of the '70s. (Except ABBA, that is; I'm such a sucker for those singing Swedes.)

# Beyond Bizarre

Then there are the creations that frighten, disturb, or just make you go "huh?"

"I am not a human!
I am a PARTY ANIMAL!"

Caught in the act?

Hey! Just what were you doing with
Sparky, anyway, Mr. Creepy Eyes?

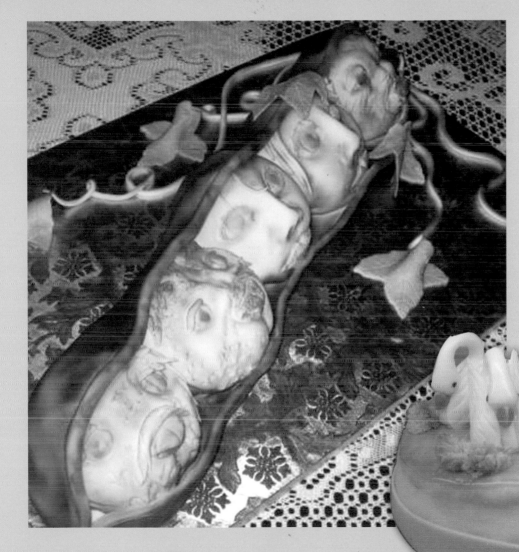

Well, this oughta put your kids off vegetables for life.

You know, I've always thought those sweet pastoral scenes with swans needed a bizarre intestinal creature to liven things up.

Anyone else want to take a guess at what Melissa is being congratulated for? Anyone? Anyone?

Nah, me neither.

Ever wonder what would happen if you ordered a cake with the instructions, "She's getting married and likes daffodils and ponies, so just make all that work"?

Nah, me neither.

You're not fooling anyone, Mr. Giant Radioactive Blob! **Now take that mask off!**

Remember, tomorrow is only a day away.

And by then, you may have recovered from seeing this cake.

*Little-known fact: before she hit the big-time with the Gorgons, Medusa went by her middle name, "Jennifer."*

# "The Italians are coming! GUARD YOUR TEETH!"

Somewhere in Kabul, there is an Italian bakery.

No, that's not the opening line for a joke; there really is an Italian bakery in Afghanistan. And since I'm fortunate enough to have readers in the military stationed all over the world, I get to share with you what the Italians in Afghanistan are baking up for our American soldiers. Check it out:

Not bad, not bad—although it looks like the cake suffered from a little friendly fire. And what's up with all the random silver balls? It reminds me of those plastic bubble mazes we had when we were kids.

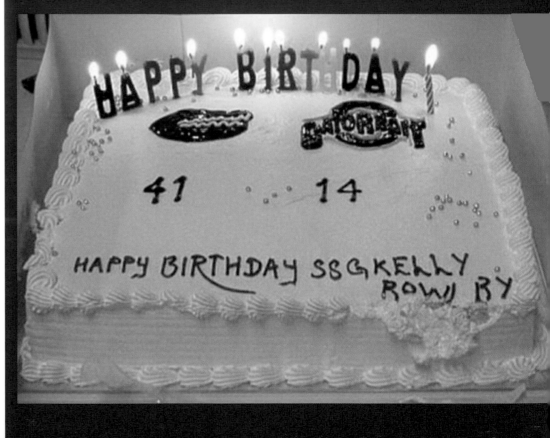

## Wait, I can explain this one! Submitter Sara writes,
"One of my guys was a reservist who had been a male stripper, hence the naked rear."

Ewwkay. Uh . . . [head tilt] do you guys see a naked rear? Kind of looks like pants to me—or shorts. Or amputated legs. Or . . . something very much NOT a naked rear. And the shading—why?

But most important: We're sending MALE STRIPPERS to Kabul?!? Dang, joining the army has never seemed so appealing—am I right, ladies? I mean, assuming this picture is not representative of what said strippers actually look like, of course.

This is like one of those old Magic Eye pictures: I simultaneously see a bear and an armadillo. But before I can decide which it is, I'm distracted by all those baffling silver balls again. I guess the Italians use them like sprinkles—metallic, BB-like, molar-breaking sprinkles.

Here's a CCC that reminds us to give thanks. Mostly for not being a chicken. Or a turkey. Or whatever the heck this is supposed to be.

"Hi-ho, Guv'na! Are those my wings behind me? 'Cuz I think they're on fire."

## This Makes Me Wonder If My Mechanic Used to Be a Baker.

Anna writes, "For my baby shower my mom ordered the cake from a local grocery store. They had given her a quote over the phone for the cake, but when she arrived to pick it up, the price was significantly higher. She had to go through several levels of management to find out that *the extra charge was for the cake to be frosted.* They informed her with all seriousness that their cakes normally came unfrosted!"

Here's an appetizing little concoction: an oozing pile of swirling buggy bits! Beehive? Oh, *behave*, you. I know all about your little euphemisms. Besides, this is clearly a representation of the classic kids film *What Happens When We Flush*. (I particularly liked the song and dance number "Don't Poo-Poo Us Poo!," didn't you?)

Speaking of which, I guess that's as good a segue as any for . . .

# The Poo Phenomenon

I've learned a lot of things from writing Cake Wrecks. I've learned that picking up the cake only thirty minutes before the party is never a good idea, fresh flowers actually *can't* fix every wedding caketastrophe, and brown icing has a spectacularly good chance of looking like poop. Maybe it's the texture, or the way decorators like to apply it in swirly little piles—I don't really know. What I *do* know is that these cakes can make even the most die-hard carb addict rethink that dessert order.

Ahh, just look at those greasy, glistening piles! You're getting hungry now, aren't you?
[nodding knowingly] I can tell.

Please tell me there's not a miniature Chihuahua around here. Because seriously, the only way this could *possibly* look more disgusting is if there were little paw prints leading up to the "leaves." Or should I call them "leavings"? [wicked grin] (Sorry, couldn't resist.) And let's not even consider the possible reasons for the blood-colored spatters, all right? I mean, we all have to eat again *someday*.

Here the baker seemed to take the labeling a little too literally.

The label:

But-R-Crème™

Chocolate

The cake:

But-R-Crème™

Chocolate

And as you can see, the blast from the expulsion has knocked Rex clean over:

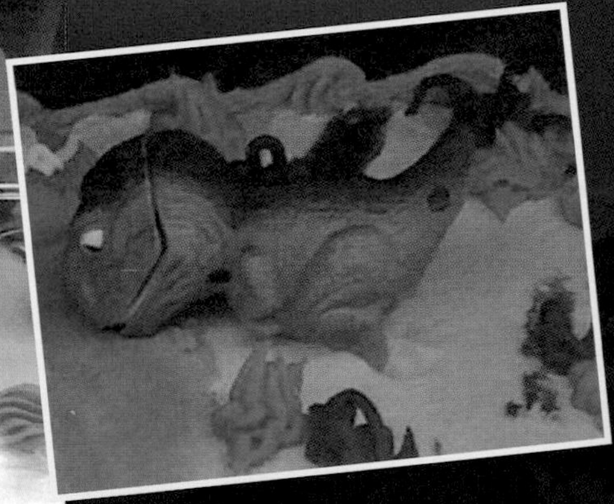

Here's another prehistoric pile:

[averting eyes] Red drippies? *Really?* Here's an idea: How about we avoid the whole poo-brown/blood-red color combo?

**Q:**

What do you think *those* are supposed to be?

**A:**

I dunno, but it sure looks like the bakers wrecked 'em.

Happy Birthday 60th Hobie.

Sometimes it's refreshing to see the simple twisty swirl. It's so much more classic than the complicated, multicolored crap you usually get these days, don't you agree?

I was about to ask what they're doing on this particular cake, but then I realized that's a centaur next to Prince Caspian there. And let's face it, girls—combining a man with a horse is going to get you three things: a toilet seat that's always up, a whole lot of innuendo-laced invitations to "ride him," and a front yard knee-deep in . . . weeds. Yeah. Because you know centaurs: so frickin' lazy.

Look at this lovely blank canvas, just waiting for your personalized greeting to complete the overall "look." Sure, yellow-swirled-poo flowers may not be ideal for birthdays, anniversaries, or other typically "happy" occasions, but there are still plenty of other options. For example:

**(1)** Have Fun at the Waste Management Plant!

**(2)** Outbreak-Free One Whole Year!

**(3)** Good Luck at Your Colonic!

**(4)** It Finally Peeled Off!

## Here's Hoping She Didn't Have to Bring Cupcakes to School

One reader e-mailed to tell me about the Most Awkward Cake Moment Ever. When she first got her period, her mother decided to celebrate the occasion with a cake. Pretty embarrassing, right? Ah, but it gets better! The mom presented the cake to her in front of the *entire family*, and written on it were the words WELCOME TO WOMANHOOD.

No matter what the occasion, your local Wreckerator has a poo design to fit it.

For Valentine's Day, tell that special someone just what they mean to you:

Specifically, "You give my bowel movement wings."

HEART SHAPE CAKE

This one reminds us to give thanks for all the *regular* people in our lives.

Yeah, I said it. How you like *them* road apples?

(Not to toot my own horn, but that was a total gas, people. A real work of art, even? Eh?)

And nothing says, "Look! I'm hugging poo!" quite like this bearer of Yuletide cheer.

Mercy, indeed.

# Go Find a Bridge to Live Under, Why Don't You?
## THE "FUN" SIDE TO INTERNET TROLLS

During her acceptance speech for a Golden Globe, Tina Fey said, "If you ever start to feel too good about yourself, they have this thing called 'the Internet.'" She then named some of her worst online critics and famously gave them permission to "suck it."

As someone who deals almost exclusively online, I was one of Tina's biggest fans that night. Hey, it's very cold in cyberspace, and putting yourself or your work out there is not for the timid. Too often you end up the target of some nincompoop who gets his jollies ripping up on others. In fact, these nincompoops are so common that we even have a special name for them: trolls.

Trolls and spam are why comment moderation, or reviewing comments before allowing them to be published, is so necessary on blogs these days. There's nothing quite so jarring to readers as the typical "you all suck, and your mothers are ugly" or "this is the stupidest post I've ever read" observations from Mr. or Mrs. Troll. Interestingly enough, most trolls seem to be named "Anonymous," too. (I can't tell you how many times I've spent a blissful afternoon imagining

"Anonymous" hooked up to an industrial-strength cattle prod.) However, like all bullies, trolls have their funny and/or clueless side, too. Here are a few examples.

### Did you hear the one about the dumb troll?

I once referenced Jackson Pollock, the famous painter, in a post. I was immediately flamed by a troll who, in all capital letters and with lots of exclamation points, informed me I was

a bigoted so-and-so.

"What next?" the troll asked. "Are you going to use [racial slur], [racial slur], or [really bad racial slur]?!?"

I'm not sure which is

more tragic: the fact that I learned three new words from that comment, or that Trolly missed out on all that rich ironic goodness.

## Say what?

Trolls excel at starting completely off-topic, nonsensical debates. If you're talking about the caterpillar in *Alice in Wonderland*, the troll will inform one and all that Lewis Carroll liked little boys. If the cake is misspelled, then one will drop in a dig against Republicans. (Or if it's tacky, the Democrats.) When everyone else is in agreement that a Playboy cake for an eight-year-old is inappropriate, count on an impassioned rant from a troll in favor of genital piercing for minors, or something equally baffling.

The worst part, though, (or best, depending on how amusing you find all of this) is that these trollish non sequiturs can really get readers' feathers in a bunch. Many will weigh in with angry retorts or lengthy explanations, not realizing that the troll in question is probably laughing his or her fool head off at the kerfuffle. Still, as long as there are no obscenities used, I just let them be. After all, as a wise man once said: There's no sense jumping in the crazy pool unless you've got a weed whacker handy. [nodding seriously] And those, my friends, are words to live by.

## Why trolls make lousy life coaches.

Just a few months after Cake Wrecks began, a troll announced that the site had officially "jumped the shark" and was no longer entertaining. A few more piled on the watery bandwagon and (anonymously, of course) assured me troll #1 was right: My talent was gone, I was trying too hard, and I might as well stop posting altogether.

At the time, CW was averaging several thousand readers a day. Today it averages over fifty thousand readers a day.

What's the saying—success is the best revenge? Yeah. I like that.

# Oops!

Hey, we all make mistakes, right? There's no shame in that. And in their defense, how many people ask decorators to write the word "birthday" on a cake, anyway?

Heppy Bartty CAROLINE

Hey, my ship has come in!

I never knew a cake inscription could be so terrifying. Hold me?

And those pesky numbers: 1st, 2nd, 3rd, 4th—they all have different endings! Who could keep them all straight, really? Far easier to just slap a "th" on them all.

**At least these Wreckerators realized they'd made a mistake, although their methods of correcting them could use a little work.**

I guess Charles didn't make it home, but fortunately Jane survived to see her name misspelled at least one more time. And we're all left to wonder: Could those corncob candles BE any bigger? (That's my Chandler Bing impression. Yeah, I'm old school that way.)

Decorators, don't like your first attempt? Then grab the brown icing! It's like Wite-Out for cakes, only brown and way, WAY more obvious.

FORETHOUGHT

It only takes a little, but dang it, that's *still* too much effort.

For those creations that don't make the cut, there is but one sad, sad fate awaiting them:

Tragic, yes, but this cake's loss is our gain. After all, what could be sweeter than munching on a hunk of someone else's rejected birthday cake? That's right:

*NOTHING*.

I like to think of it as sharing in a stranger's celebration, only without all that pesky police intervention and bothersome restraining orders. [stuffing face with cake] Hafpfy birfay, 'on! Got 'ny milk?

Here's a save for the history books. Why, I can almost feel the confidence radiating from that sincere, heartfelt inscription.

Kristin is your typical super-mom: She stayed up all night baking her daughter's fourth-birthday cake. So naturally she was shocked when, upon seeing her lovely pink-flowered cake, the little girl burst into tears. Turns out Kristin had accidentally put a number 3 on the cake, and the poor tot thought this meant she would have to repeat her third year of life all over again. (If only it *did* work that way, my dear . . .)

In an effort to calm the child, Kristin grabbed the nearest tube of frosting and hastily put a giant 4 over the 3. The girl kept crying. "*Now* what's wrong?" Kristin asked, only to be told she "made the number wrong."

After more tears and corrections, the cake looked like this, and Kristin assures me she will never again forget how old her only child is.

## Whoppie:

a cross between a Whopper and a whoopie cushion. Emits that fresh, flame-broiled smell when sat upon.

Ah, sweet, sweet irony. Perhaps someone should consider summer school?

SO close.

The relative Wreckiness of this cake depends on what your definition of "is" is.

She's either just changed her name or has a serious medical condition. Either way, you'll bring home brownies if you know what's good for you.

Who?

Did you know that icing hardens over time? Yep. So after, say, a whole year,
your average icing would be so rock-solid that you'd need a chisel to remove it.

Why do I bring that up?

Oh, no reason.

"No, really, I'm sure it tastes great. I'm just a little skeptical of your 'baked fresh' claim, is all."

Like many of you, I used to think decorators who couldn't manage even the simplest inscriptions were idiots. Now, thanks to copious amounts of *Boston Legal* episodes, I know some of them are simply suffering from the affliction known as "word salad" (the rest are, in fact, idiots). So instead of deriding these decorators, I now advise them to seek help. Right after they get someone *else* to fix my cake, that is.

I looked it up, and "lave" means "wash."

See, *now* this cake makes sense.

Um, old enough to know how to spell "you're"?

"Hey, Sarah, did you phone in that order for Jonathan's birthday cake?"

"No, I had Mary H. do it."

"Oh no, really?"

"Why, what's wrong with that?"

"Oops, here she comes now. Er, hi, Mary!"

"Hey, Crythtal! Hey, Tharah! How'th it goin'?"

"Good, Mary. Thanks for asking. And, uh, thanks for ordering the cake for me."

"No thweat! I wath glad to do it! Well, thee you two at the party!"

As I understand it, 100th birthday parties are a celebration of *life*, right?

## Why We Need a Patron Saint of Cakes

Katya writes:

I was supposed to bring a cake to a party for a priest, celebrating the anniversary of his ordination. I wanted the cake to say "Happy Anniversary, Father Pat." Well, lo and behold, the clerk at the bakery was a surly teenager. Warning bells went off in my head, but I pressed on regardless. I told her the message I wanted, and she looked at me like I was reciting ancient Greek. So I spoke as if to an imbecile (foreshadowing, perhaps?): "Hap-py Ann-i-ver-sa-ry."

"How many 'n's in 'anniversary'?" she asked.

"Two," I replied.

She got out her tube of icing and proceeded to write "Happy" with only one "p." I corrected her, whereupon she squashed another "p" into the word. Next she wrote the "a" for "anniversary" before stopping, confused.

"I need to write this down," she said.

"Fine, fine," I replied, and spelled out A-N-N-I-V-E-R-S-A-R-Y. She copied it down diligently, or so I thought; it was difficult to see from my vantage point.

"Now write 'Father Pat,'" I instructed.

She stared at me defiantly. "How do you spell 'father'?"

I should have just run away screaming.

When I got the cake home and discovered the extent of the destruction, it was immediately chucked. And *that* is why I normally do my own baking.

# And a Nappy
# BLOB BLOB TO YOU!

Or: To Turn a Birthday Wreck into Birthday Fun, Just Add Alcohol.

**Beth writes:**

"My friend brought this cake to my birthday party. At first, I was ecstatic to have a friend so considerate, but after she unveiled the cake both of our faces fell. Instead of 'Happy Birthday, Beth!' the cake read 'Nappy' followed by two large blobs of icing.

"Luckily, we were at a location that supplied copious amounts of overpriced alcohol, so what could have been a birthday disaster turned into a huge joke complete with people shouting 'Nappy blob blob!' at me from across the venue."

# Wedding Wrecks

There's nothing quite so tragic as the Wedding Wreck. After all, this is the cake the bride daydreamed about when she was little, agonized over with the wedding planner, and ultimately ordered with starry-eyed hopes of a fairy-tale happily ever after. So naturally, when she gets something like this:

Well, it's pretty darn funny.

No, no, of course I don't mean *funny* funny. I mean gut-wrenchingly awful, with a side of snickering schadenfreude, that's all! See, nothing insensitive about that, right?

Still, I think it's only right that we should gain a little enlightenment from these Wrecks, in addition to entertainment. So here are some helpful tips I've gleaned after seeing more than my fair share of these Big Day caketastrophes.

# 1.

*Fresh flowers are far less so after hour 16.*

Yes, nothing symbolizes the beginning of a new life together with the one you love quite like shriveled old roses. This look is particularly hazardous for those of you marrying later in life; it only takes one overheard "bloom off the rose" remark to cause a Bridezilla meltdown of *Weddings Gone Wild* proportions. Trust me.

Spare your guests the gore. If you don't talk to your baker about floral shelf life, who will?

# 2.

*The word "periwinkle" can mean many things to many people. Also, some decorators are color-blind.*

*Now there's a color match made in my blue heaven.*

Some bakeries have color translation charts in the back. On these charts, words like "periwinkle," "robin's egg," and "azure" are all neatly typed under the heading "BLUE." So unless you're content with your "chartreuse" ending up a wee bit more "Leprechaun Vomit," ask to see the actual icing color.

Here a "soft leaf green" quite literally makes everything else pale in comparison. And those black clumps, resembling so much doggy doo in the grass? Why, those are the "wine-colored" roses, of course!

Whoopsie!

# 3.

*When ordering a "whimsically leaning" cake, make sure the baker has a basic understanding of architecture.*

What remains relatively upright in Pisa will not necessarily do so in sponge cake. Granted, these are the Wedding Wrecks in the more catastrophic sense, but whether Uncle Bob bumped the table or your baker was just an incompetent ninny is for you (and your lawyers) to decide.

## 4.

### Consider the weather.

Any baker will tell you cakes and humidity don't mix. Heat is a no-no, too. So if you're getting married in a swamp and you order a hand-painted cake, don't be surprised if you end up with something that looks like Tammy Faye after a revival.

*(What, too dated? See, she wore a lot of mascara, and she cried a lot . . . Um, well, it kind of loses something when you explain it.)*

# 5.

*Play-Doh is neither elegant nor appetizing.*

If your cake decorations look like they came from craft time at the local preschool, odds are your baker missed the mark. And if you *must* order brown icing, then please, for the love of all things edible, *don't* have it arranged in long, poo-like logs!

# 6.

## Some Wrecks are your fault.

Yes, you. I'm sorry, but the time has come for us to face the ugly truth: Some Wrecks are exactly what the customer asked for. Like this one:

This is a *wedding* cake, people. A wedding cake! With camo! And dolphins! And little plastic army men! It's insane! And I can't stop using exclamation marks!

And yet, I'm told the bride was "thrilled" with this cake, so we can only assume it's just what she wanted. Can't blame the baker there, now, can we? Nope. See, some decorators will do anything you want, if the price is right. (Okay, not *anything*. Perv.) However, just because they *can* do something doesn't mean they *should*. The answer "because it is there" does not suffice for a life-sized, glitter-encrusted, tutu-wearing unicorn cake, complete with balloon arch. It just doesn't. Unless you're five. At which point, save me a slice?

## 7.

# Location, location, location.

## 'Nuff said.

Before some of you start complaining about the "obscenity" in this photo, I'd like to remind you that having a cupcake tower instead of a wedding cake isn't *technically* obscene. It just looks silly when you and your new spouse pose next to it with a big cake knife.

## 9.

*When all seems lost,
take heart; your wedding cake
could end up a fan favorite
on Cake Wrecks.*

❧◆❧

**The setup:**

The bride wanted her cake to have a tartan border and accents. You know, tartan—that plaid material on a kilt?—and even provided her baker with an inspiration photo from a fancy wedding magazine. I can't show you the picture here due to copyright muckety-muck, so just imagine a white tiered cake with a somewhat elegant *Braveheart* vibe.

**The letdown:**

Well, for *some* reason the happy couple took issue with what the paid, "professional" baker provided on their wedding day:

But you know couples these days: *so* picky!

I mean, sure, the cake is collapsed in on itself, slumped over to one side, and channeling a bit more Bob Marley than William Wallace, but besides all that I'd say the decorator was bang on, wouldn't you?

Okay, okay, if you wanted to get *picky* about it, I guess that crack in the bottom—the one you can see the cake through?—that probably should have been iced over. Oh, and the red stripe might look a little nicer if it were one continuous line—or for that matter, if the line were straight. (Perhaps a little too much Red Stripe was consumed before icing the red stripe, eh? *Eh?* Come on, that was freakin' hilarious, people. Bob Marley? Jamaican beer? Booya!)

Come to think of it, maybe that mass of squiggles in the midsection isn't the *best* example of plaid I've ever seen, either. [tilting head to one side] Huh. Yeah. Okay, you got me: I can sort of see why the bride sued.

Just when all seems lost, the cake
unleashes its secret weapon:
the rocket roses. Soon the silverware
will retreat, off to hunt easier,
more vulnerable prey.

Why? Because it is there.

And because I grew up on
*The Far Side*.

# Groom's
# CAKES

The groom's cake is the rather curious wedding tradition of giving the husband-to-be absolute stylistic control over approximately two square feet of his own wedding reception. We women generally allow this foolishness for two reasons:

1. "He's just so cute when he begs!"
2. "How badly can a single cake screw up my 'Love of a Lifetime' theme, anyway?"

Unfortunately, some men take this as a personal challenge.

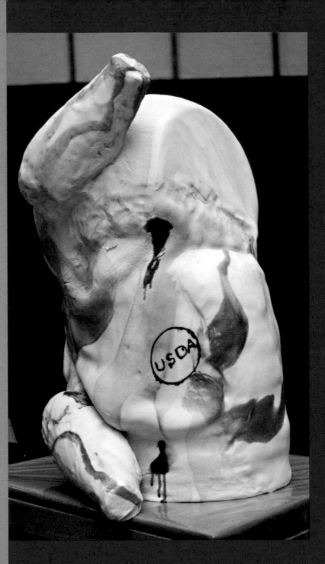

## Aaand now we know.

Yes, this oozing slab of "beef" really is a groom's cake. I'd love to include the photo of the bride looking on while the groom cuts it, but I feel I must protect the identities of the innocent.

Some guys are mercifully subtle: These "bacon" strips could almost pass for bubble tape—and they go nicely with the pink roses, don't you think?

This is also a groom's cake, but I do have some good news:

1. Those are NOT red Bic lighters as I initially thought. They're shotgun shells. (Phew!)
2. For those of you who've always wondered what it would be like to suck frosting off of feathers: surprise! You're about to find out!
3. I just saved a bunch of money on my car insurance. (Haha! It just *never* gets old, does it?)

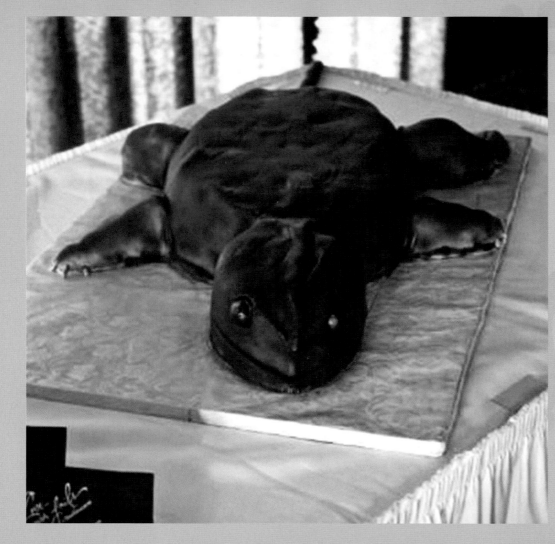

Oh, and speaking of geckos . . .

That's what this is supposed to be.

"It's . . . *looking* at me."

"He's an ugly little spud, isn't he?"

"I think he can hear you, Ray."

Considering that most fish groom's cakes I see look like they just finished wriggling, I suppose I should be grateful that this one looks more like a decaying pickle. Then again, that raises an interesting question: Which would you rather eat: a slimy whole fish or a fuzzy, month-old pickle? Use that as an icebreaker at your next party and I *guarantee* you'll get people talking.*

* Why, last night I had folks yakking a mile a minute—mostly about how they might have left the oven on and so had to leave immediately, but still, the conversation up to that point was positively *riveting*.

Of course, no discussion on groom's cakes would be complete without one of these:

I know it's hard to recognize, considering you're not in a car and he's not spread over five feet of asphalt, but that's an armadillo. Crafting cakes made to look like these scaly roadkill fodder became all the rage after a similar cake was featured in the movie *Steel Magnolias*. Since then guys have added their own unique spin on the tradition by often adding bullet holes, bloody gashes, and/or tire treads through the middle of the armadillo—to help their guests recognize it, perhaps?

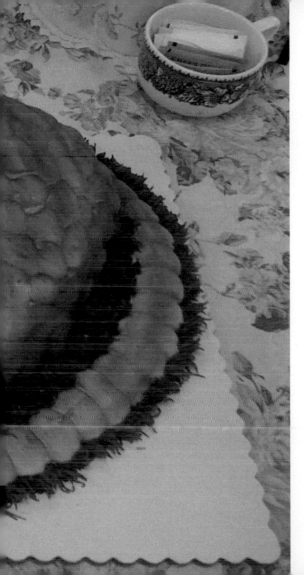

Of course, if you're going to have a cake that looks like an animal—dead or otherwise—you *know* you have to make it out of red velvet. It's one of the unwritten rules of cake decorating. And I wouldn't mind so much, either, except that everyone who sees an animal or person-shaped cake and then makes the crack, "Hey, you think they made it out of red velvet? Bwahahah!" thinks he is the very *first* person to do so.

[rubbing temples] "Ah, yes: red velvet. Good one. Haven't heard that in, oh, at least an hour or so. Look, I'm just off to jab myself in the eyes for a bit, if it's all the same to you . . ."

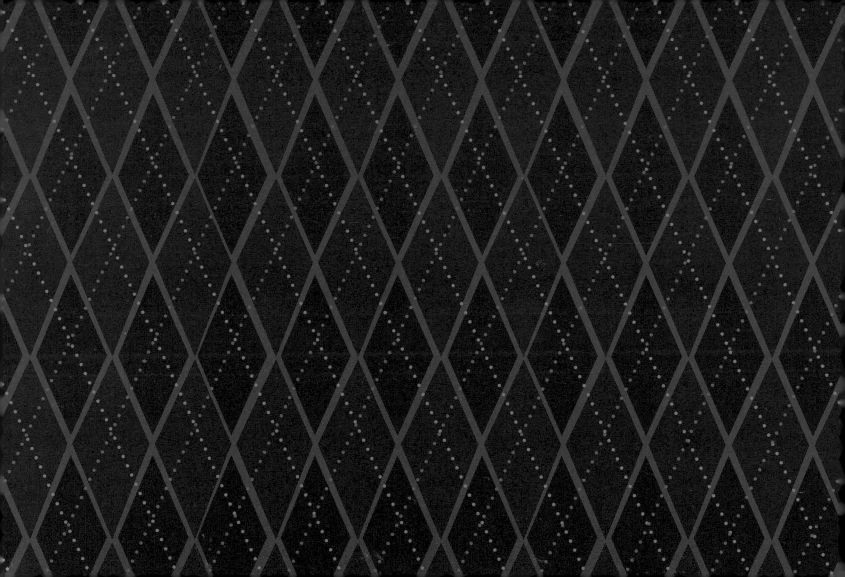

# What's *That* Supposed to Mean?

There are innocent mistakes, and then there are the ones that make you wonder . . .

I DIDN'T LIKE YOU THAT MUCH ANYWAY

Have the grandkids finally had enough?

*Psst,* hey, guys: "Brandy's" new identity is never gonna stick if you keep putting her name in quotes.

She's not the only one, though; a lot of folks in the Witness Protection Program have been outed this way.

Looks like "Deb" may have to pay those gambling debts after all.

Nancy is a librarian, so her husband asked the baker to put something book-related on her birthday cake. Unfortunately, this was the extent of the decorator's creativity:

# Is near?

Remember, Nancy, this isn't so much a celebration of your *life* as it is a commemoration of your being one year closer to death. You know, another chapter of your life coming to a close? The final pages being turned? That's all she wrote? *The End*?

Oh, and look: Aunt Jillian sent over some headstone brochures! Aw, isn't she just the *sweetest*?

Here's a tip gleaned from years of family gatherings: The second someone asks "What's *that* supposed to mean?" it's time to leave. Trust me.

# What's In
# A NAME?

Wow, Chris wasn't kidding when he said he got a big promotion! In fact, I'm not so sure he needs the luck now, "yood" or otherwise.

For Debbie's birthday her officemates ordered her favorite cake: strawberry glazed.
Since they figured the decorator wouldn't be able to write her name on top of the fruit glaze,
though, they asked for a "Happy Birthday" pick to be stuck in the cake instead.

Hey, Debbie, guess who's getting a new nickname?

It could have been worse, though. Debbie's first cake *ever* could have saddled her with this:

Imagine going through life with *that* story hanging over your head. Every time you start to glisten even a little, your folks would be there reminding you of that "oh-so-hilarious" shower cake. [shaking head] Poor little Sweaty—er, sorry, I mean *Swetty*.

No, the baby's last name actually *wasn't* "Swetty"—this was supposed to read "Sweetie."

Although it did get me thinking: Say her last name really *was* Swetty. And say she grew up and got engaged to someone with the last name "Hott." How awesome would that be?!? C'mon, the "Hott & Swetty Wedding"? You know *those* invitations would never get thrown out.

HUGE ME

Here's a frosted Freudian slip if I've ever seen one.

Stephen's girlfriend got him this for Valentine's Day, and claims she didn't notice the error until after she'd purchased it. Riiiight. We'll just go with that, shall we, Stephen? [wink wink]

Best Wishes Melissa, The Bribe To Be

This one's a bit less complimentary.

Well, at least she gets a cake out of it.

For those of you who don't think punctuation is a big deal, let me assure you: It is.

When in doubt it's always key to appear confident, I always say.* Especially since there can be some massive repercussions from confusing a question mark with an exclamation mark.

"I love you, Betsy!"
"I love you, too . . . Mark?"

See? You know that can't end well.

*At least, I *think* I do . . .

When northern California was being ravaged by massive wildfires, one local bakery sprang into action. This band of brave decorators quickly and heroically set about crafting cakes to show their unwavering support and heartfelt sympathy for their northern California neighbors.

The cakes, which they prepared by the rack-full, looked like this:

And I don't know about you, but I'm feelin' the love. Like a hunk-a-hunk of *burnin'* love!

Still, despite the demonic deer staring into the depths of my soul (and thusly creeping me the heck out), I'm actually quite impressed. Sure, the smoke column on the side is a little odd, but I like the idea of using sprinkles for ash. It's chipper.

When questioned, one decorator explained that these were "fall" cakes. It was June at the time.

Does it get Wreckier than that, you ask? Aw, shucks, you know it does!

This was supposed to say, "Happy Birthday, You Old Bastard!" so I'm going to go out on a limb here and guess the wonky heart was the *decorator's* idea.

"Let's see, demonic deer, unintelligible greeting, hmm . . . it still needs *something* . . ."

Oh, wait, do you suppose that smoke column on the first cake was supposed to be a *tree*? Huh. Well, I guess if all the leaves were burned off . . .

# CRAZY CONTROVERSIES YOU NEVER KNEW CAKE COULD CREATE

You would think that few things could be more innocent than cake, wouldn't you? I mean, it's a sweet baked good served at parties—what could stir up strife there? Ah, well, allow me to illumine you.

## What's in a Name?

You may remember this one, since it was all over the news just before Christmas 2008: A grocery store bakery refused to write a little boy's name on his birthday cake. Why? Because his name was Adolf Hitler Campbell, and his parents insisted his *entire* name be on the cake.

I posted the story on Wrecks, and you would not *believe* the resulting public outcry—or then again, maybe you would. From debates over freedom of speech to accusations of child abuse to ranting about the tyranny of some secret society of Jews that evidently runs the country, people certainly got their panties in a bunch over this story. So the moral is: If you want endless amounts of free publicity, just name your kid after a ruthless mass murderer. Yep, thaaat oughta do it.

(And by the way, super-secret society: I'm Jewish on my mother's side, and have not yet received my *How to Rule the World* handbook, membership pass, and decoder ring. Who exactly do I contact about this?)

## For the Love of Betty Crocker, Don't Tick Off the Diabetics!

I'm actually still a bit chagrined about this one, since *I'm* the one who caused the controversy. I posted a cake shaped like an insulin pen on Wrecks and then made a crack about how ironic it was, considering a diabetic's foot could "fall off" after eating it. Now, given the amount of sarcasm normally bandied about on Wrecks, and the fact that I admitted in the post that I have a family history of diabetes and am at high risk of developing it myself, you might think that folks would take this comment with a grain of "I have a sense of humor" salt. If you did, however, you would be wrong. So, *so* wrong.

By midafternoon of the day in question, I was called more names and virtually yelled at by more people than I think I ever have been, before or since. And while we're on the subject: Did *you* know that diabetics can eat sugar? And that perpetuating misinformation about a deadly disease is both cruel *and* insensitive? And that anyone who *does* perpetuate said misinformation deserves to either have her own foot chopped off or to sit idly by while watching a loved one succumb to the agonies of an insulin-deficient death? Well? *Did you*?

Of course, I don't think it helped matters when another reader (and personal friend of mine) commented "Ignore the haters, Jen. They're just grumpy 'cuz they can't have any cake." So. Not. Helping.

Needless to say, the entire post was removed by day's end.

## "You can tell this is fake because the shadows are all wrong."

### Photoshop: the skeptic's answer to everything

I don't always post cakes that are misspelled or ugly; some are just plain creepy. One of my favorites in this category was a groom's cake shaped like the groom's *head* wearing a football helmet. What made it particularly gruesome, though, was the dead-eyed, somber expression on the almost-unbelievably realistic face. I'm pretty sure the baker printed the face using edible photo paper, but since a lot of folks out there don't know such a thing exists, many called foul, saying it was Photoshopped. This wouldn't have bothered me so much, except that I felt the actual *writing* of the post was some of my best to date, and here everyone was ignoring my genius commentary and instead squabbling over whether the cake was "real." [crossing arms and pouting] Hmph.

The head cake taught me a valuable lesson, though: For Wrecks that I knew were going to get a huge reaction on their own, I learned to not spend too much time or space on commentary. Far better to let a Wreck that can speak for itself do so. I also learned that controversy almost always equals publicity: The next cake that caused a "real or fake" debate landed Wrecks on a huge consumer advocacy blog, which then resulted in a massive readership boost. That almost made up for all the readers calling me a gullible idiot for posting it. Almost. (I'm sensitive, all right? So sue me. [I meant that figuratively; please don't sue me.])

[nodding sagely] Aren't we all, my friends—aren't we all.

Cake has been used to impart some very painful truths . . .

I Don't Want to go Out With You Anymore

on *both* sides of the aisle:

I DIDN'T LIKE YOU THAT MUCH ANYWAY

Then again,
everyone handles
being dumped
differently.

Go Die in a car
fire

# Ouch.

Divorce cakes are really gaining in popularity these days (yes, this was a cake celebrating cutting the knot). Think divorce is an odd occasion for cake? [flapping fingers dismissively] Pshaw! That's nothing! From "Thanks for Posting Bail" to "Congrats on Your Vasectomy," I've seen enough iced inscriptions to know that cake is the perfect vehicle for every off-the-wall event Hallmark's never dreamed of.

See?

## Just be glad she's laughing, Dave.

Dave and Phyllis were the victims of an abbreviation complication on their thirty-fifth anniversary cake. Their friends asked for a simple "Happy 35th Anniversary, Dave and Phyllis," but the baker must have abbreviated "anniversary" on the order form.

Fortunately, Phyllis took her name being misspelled and the addition of another woman to the marriage all in stride. In fact, I hear that today, sixteen years later, she and Dave still make cracks about his "other wife, Ann."

# Nuthin' to See Here . . .

It's like the story of the emperor with no clothes; who's going to be the first to admit seeing something wrong with this cake?

What, no one? Here, what if we turn it around . . .

Bonne Fête
Sarah-Maude
2 ans !

Those balloons remind you of, oh, I dunno . . . anything at all?

If you're laughing right now, good news! You are gonna LOVE this chapter. If you're *not* laughing, however, then may I recommend the excellent Run Home Wrecks on page 129?

You can chalk it up to too many *Are You Being Served?* reruns or pure juvenile gutter-minded humor if you must, but I don't think I'm the only one to find the odd icing innuendo pretty darn funny.

Sure, most of these are completely unintentional and were probably made by sweet, innocent grandmothers who wouldn't see the problem if you spelled it out for them with a laser pointer and a flow chart. Others could be more insidious, but it's hard to say. After all, in order to ask you'd have to admit to seeing something *other* than a balloon. Which I don't. Why, do you?

It's not surprising that carrots would be big offenders in this category. Still, some go above and beyond the call of duty, if you catch my wink-wink-nudge-nudge-say-no-more drift.

Suurrre it's a carrot. With a fig leaf.

Show-off.

Over on the other end of the gender spectrum:

"Pumkin Fun"? Methinks this bakery needs a dictionary on-site. And maybe—just shooting this out there—another mandatory sexual harassment seminar.

And if you think I have a *cake* for a mandatory sexual harassment seminar, then *ding-ding-ding!* You are correct, sir!

And this *clearly* calls for a celebration!

I just love that someone—either the customer or the decorator—felt that "sexual harassment" needed to be illustrated. And I realize that the decorator can't be expected to be Picasso or anything, but check out how far the girl's feet are off the ground. Either that was the Spank Heard 'Round the World, or she's on an invisible step while Chuckles there digs for gold.

## Nice nuts.

Sure, I get it; it's a family tree. The big acorns are the grandparents, and the little ones are the kids and grandkids.

However . . .

Did no one think that placing two *giant nuts* at the base of a tall wood tree that's showering the ground with its seed might bring . . . oh, I dunno . . . *other* metaphors to mind?

Just to be clear, this is a gavel:

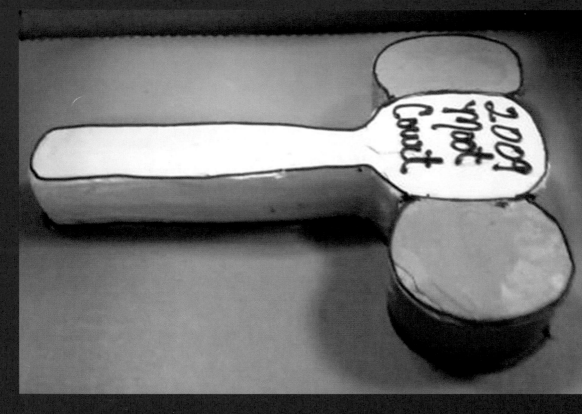

You know, that thing judges use to pound, er, I mean, to *bang* . . . wait, no . . . That is, it's the wood . . . hammer thing . . . used in courts. Yeah. A gavel. A rounded, flesh-tone gavel.

(Phew! Glad I got through that without saying anything suggestive!)

Right, so that's a gavel.

These, on the other hand, are NOT gavels:

The difference evidently lies in the bright pink, yellow, and chocolate coatings.
That, and the classy plastic bucket display system. Good to know, good to know.

Okay, now we're just being childish. Really. So stop laughing already.

Meredith was throwing a bachelorette party, and the bride had only one request:

Also according to Meredith, there's nothing quite so blush-inducing as having the following conversation with the sweet elderly man with the heavy foreign accent taking the order:

"Not . . . a . . . pen . . . is cake?"

"Um, no. Not a PENIS cake. P-E-N-I-S. One word."

"Ohhhh, okay . . . PENIS, P-E-N-I-S."

Hey, he *did* get it right!

*Yowza.* Walt is spinning in his cryogenically preserved chamber right now.

And how do you leave off an entire word, anyway? Did the decorator just get distracted at the last . . .

*Ooh look, shiny!*

May All Your Dreams Come

# Sweet
# SEDUCTION

"Girl, you lookin' *fine*. Why don't you come over here, and give Daddy a li'l sugar?"

"Check it. I've got a ca-*razy* polar-bear-skin rug for us to lounge on, and some suh-*weet* champagne glasses the size of water coolers, filled with extra shag. Not that we'll be *needing* any extra shag, of course." [eyebrow waggle] "That's right, pudd'n: I may not be for sale, but you can still be my 'lucky lady,' if you *know* what I mean."

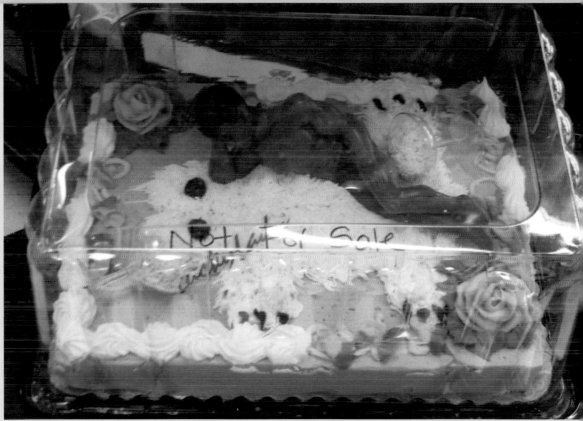

"Oh, dang, girl, I see you've already *got* a rug and water-cooler glasses. But you know what you don't have, my minxy little meow? Me, doing leg lifts."

"That's right. You dig it? This cracked concrete floor isn't the *only* thing that's rock-hard around here, if you get me." [wink wink] "Yeah, these here abs are *tight*!"

"Aw, girl, did you invite a friend? Hey, not that I don't admire a little *initiative*, my sugar-fried dumpling, but I'm more of a one-woman show, if you know what I'm sayin'. This here bottle overflows for you and you *alone*, my precious pan-seared custard cup. Mm-hmm, that's right. Oh, and I've got champagne, too." [brandishing bottle]

"Aw yeeeah, now THIS is what I'm talkin' 'bout. You, a bondage bra, me, some latex floor coverings, a weird adobe fireplace thing . . . yeah, it's all workin'. In fact, I think I'm ready to fire your place, if you . . . . oh. You do?

"Well, ok then."

# Run Home Wrecks

The nice thing about sports cakes is you've got a better-than-average shot at making them recognizable. Hey, most of the balls are round, right? Well, most *cakes* are round! How can you screw that up?

Ah. I guess like that.

You've got to admire the thought process that results in a cake like this, though. I mean, it's a plastic basketball dome on what I assume is meant to be . . . a . . . flattened basketball? Or maybe a *melting* basketball? Could this be a Dali fan at work?

It's a brown swirly mass with red stitches. Mmmmmkay . . .
Oh, but look! It has a little football on it! So obviously it's . . . a football! Yeah! Woo! Go "Boomer Sooner"!

Wait. What?

"Hey, kids! Wanna see a neat trick? Watch as I turn this *white* icing a dark singed brown!"
[lowering goggles and igniting blow torch] "You might want to stand back a little, now . . . "

"It's NAHT a TOOmur." (It's worse: a friggin' Cupcake Cake.) Love the little green cupcake at the bottom, too. It's all, "Hey, I totally fit in here. See? I'm like, grassy!"

Okay, let's get away from all these dreaded CCCs for a bit. Surely a sports sheet cake will look better?

[sound of head hitting desk repeatedly]

Perspective, thou art a cold, cruel mistress.

Sure, I know it's *supposed* to be a basketball, but I prefer to think of it as a frog straddling a grapefruit. *You* may choose to see a UFO with racing stripes, or a Plinko chip from *The Price Is Right*—hey, I'm not here to judge.

And lo, the clouds did part, and the lightning did zag, and the Lord said, "Maketh thine 'B ball' swirlieth, that no mortal eye may deciphereth its form." And lo, the decorator did maketh it so. Eth.

I suppose I should mention here that I know absolutely *nothing* about sports.
Consequently, I feel a special kinship with these bakers.

Here X marks
the spot for some
run home fun!

It is with great
chagrin that I tell
you it took me a
few minutes to "get"
what was wrong
with this cake.
Then I spotted the
doily. C'mon, a girly
lace doily under a
baseball field cake?
Really? Hah—even *I*
know *that's* wrong!

I think the problem here is mostly one of scale.

No, wait, sorry . . . [touching earpiece] I'm now hearing reports that this is the wrong ball.
Repeat: This is the *wrong ball*. Geez, sports are complicated! I'm starting to feel sorry
for these poor decorators, expected to keep all their balls straight.

What? Why's everyone looking at me like that?

Oh, wait, I know this one! Yeah, I can totally tell you what's wrong with this CCC!

Well, first, it's a CCC. But also, those funky shoes look like they're about to kick *massively* disproportionate baseballs. Which is totally wrong! Everyone knows you have to *hit* baseballs with a *base*. Duh! [shaking head] You know, once you understand the basic concepts, this stuff really isn't all that hard to remember, guys. So you should, like, totally get with the program.

Hmm. Looks more like an asterisk.

This decorator obeys the letter of the law, if not the spirit:

See? It's a baseball diamond.

Wait for it . . . waaaait for it . . . Ah, there's the groan! Now we can move on.

Michele's six-year-old niece desperately wanted a *High School Musical* cake for her birthday. So naturally, Michele and her mom began telling the girl what she was going to *get* was a pink tarantula cake. Just 'cuz. And then they followed through on their threat:

Okay, so they *also* had the requested *HSM* cake, which they did serve . . . eventually. Heheheh.

I'm torn between feeling outraged on behalf of the niece and wishing I had a niece to do this to. Hey, everybody needs something to talk about in therapy later, right? Besides, I've *seen* those *High School Musical* cakes, and I bet the pink tarantula looked way better.

# Baby Bottoms Up!

I don't know what it is about a new life being brought into the world that makes so many women turn graphically cannibalistic, but a lot of the baby shower cakes out there would make the Donner Party feel right at home.

Run for your lives!

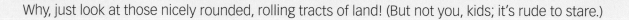

Why, just look at those nicely rounded, rolling tracts of land! (But not you, kids; it's rude to stare.)

Oh, and hey, there's a cake to match!

## "Okay, Doris, come on over here and let's com-paaare!" [singsong voice]

"My, *someone* took a little artistic license, didn't they? Oh, I'm just kidding, sweetie; you look absolutely . . . er . . . *fabulously* . . . plumped out!

"Oh, now honey, don't cry! I meant that in a *good* way! Here, I know what'll cheer you up: How about a niiice slice of boobie, hmm?"

As I mentioned in "What's a Wreck?," not all Wrecks are poorly made. This one, for example, is gorgeous; I just find the *concept* of a torso cake Wrecky.

I'm pretty sure this was the first "nice" cake I chose to poke fun at on the blog, and it was also the first to have its creator *find* it on the blog. Fortunately, Kate (the baker) found her cake's entry hilarious, and has been a fantastic sport about the whole thing. She even introduced me to the term "wachungas," which I think we can all agree is a fantastic alternative to the usual term for female appendages: golden bozos.

As belly cakes grew in popularity, folks began to realize that they were missing something. No, not limbs or a head—who needs those? No, I'm talking about something absolutely *vital* for all-female celebrations of impending childbirth:

# sex appeal.

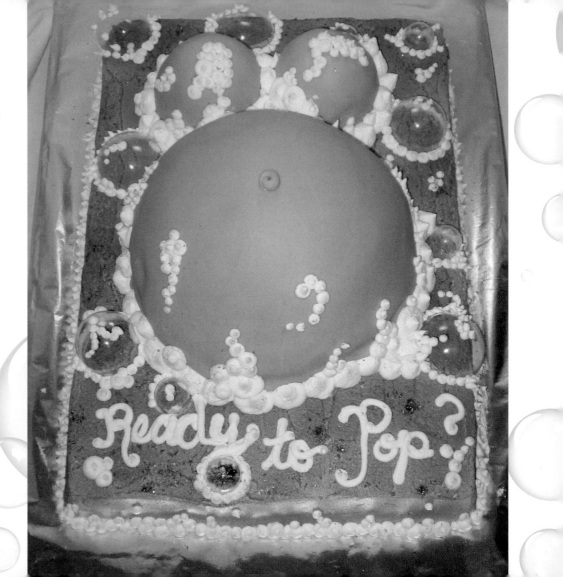

Yes, not only is this steamy little number sure to please all the . . . er . . . girls?—it also has an *extra special* feature you're just going to *love*. Here, I'll let Susan, the baker, tell you about it:

"The highlight was that the belly was filled with custard with a *tacky little plastic baby inside*. When the mom-to-be cut into the cake she had to use forceps (kitchen tongs) to remove the plastic baby. Honestly, it was VERY funny at the time."

I have no doubt, Susan. Why, the very thought of those "miracle of birth" videos made edible is causing me to have some absolutely *hysterical* convulsions over here. Just remember: It's all fun and games 'til Mom-to-Be's in the delivery room talking smack and brandishing a pair of kitchen tongs, mmkay?

Belly cakes are really nothing compared to *baby* cakes, though. Because if eating Mom's belly is good, then eating the baby is grrrreat!

Consider this tasty little morsel:

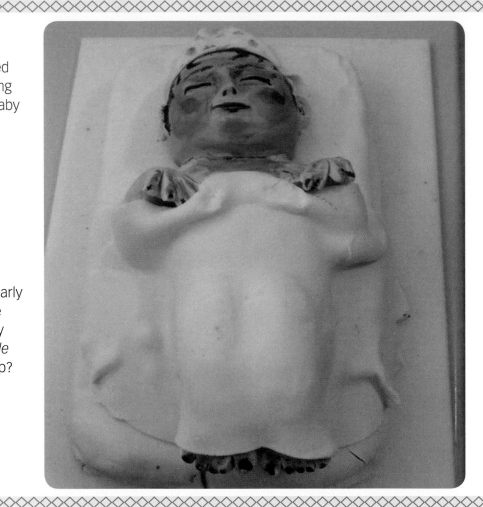

Sure, the dear may look a bit more "dearly departed," what with the white marble slab, black toenails, and various bloody streaks, but *lookit that adowable widdle face*! Don't you just want to eat it all up?

Oh, pish tosh. You say "in pain,"
I say "a little gas." Either way,
that expression screams

*"scrumptious"* !

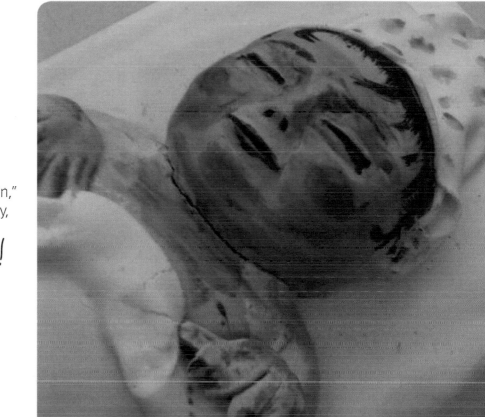

This one, on the other hand, is just screaming. (Or is that the voice in my head again?)

Call it a quirk, but I've always preferred to win any staring contests I have with my food.

Now some of you will point out—and rightly so—that this is a display cake, and therefore was not (and has not been) eaten. However, consider this: That petrified, chipped-up baby with the vacant stare is intended to entice onlookers to purchase a cake *just like it*. And since it's evidently been in that window for some time, it must *actually be working*. Tell me that's not scary. Go on.

But wait, there's more! Keep reading and in the next five minutes you'll *also* get the lowdown on the pinnacle of baby shower cakedom: the Bisected Baby Butt Cake! You've tried the *breast*, now try the *best* with this tasty, chocolate-mousse-filled treat!

What do you mean, "Where's the other half?" The diaper is the best part! Didn't you hear me say it was filled with chocolate mousse? Geez, what more could you want?

# Bakers with Humor,
## OR WHY I HAVEN'T BEEN LYNCHED YET

You wouldn't think that writing a blog—and now a book—called *Cake Wrecks* would exactly endear me to the professional baking community, would you? And yet, I'm continually delighted at how quickly and warmly bakers—both pros and amateurs alike—have embraced my goofy little cake blog. Some of the pros even have enough of a sense of humor about it that they *submit their own cakes*. Yes, really! Others have given me blanket permission to use any cake from their site that I like. Now how's that for trust? I can't think of a higher compliment, really.

Not everyone loves me, of course, but of over a thousand photos currently posted online I've had only four or five elicit complaints from the bakers responsible. Of those "complaints," only one or two would qualify as actual "hate mail." (For the record: I remove any photo a baker asks me to.) And while most pro bakers I hear from tell me they live in fear of ending up on Wrecks, the ones who do often laugh and tell me they don't mind so much. I like to think this is because I keep the humor on Wrecks lighthearted, and steer clear of personal attacks or mean-spirited insults. I see

Wrecks as a kind of good-natured razzing among friends, and it's always been my hope that bakers would see it that way, too.

I also have a genuine love for the world of cake art, which is why I feature amazing NON-Wrecks every Sunday on the blog. These "Sunday Sweets" are the flip side to Cake Wrecks, and hopefully they show decorators that I'm just as happy to applaud their triumphs as poke fun at their goof-ups. Good cakes may not be as funny, but they're still fun to look at. Besides, they add a healthy dose of perspective; I can't have readers getting so acclimated to Wreckage that they come to expect it as the norm, now, can I?

All right, fine, how about this one?

See, here the little tyke isn't cut in half: S/he's just buried upside-down in the cake. Happy?

Remember how I said some bakers submit their own cakes? Well, I've gotta throw some special love out to Zillycakes' famous Zilly Rosen and her assistant Mo McKenna for allowing me to give these *half-assed* cakes of theirs the *bum rap*. Girls, your talent is exceeded only by your senses of humor, so thanks—from the *bottom* of my heart.

Mercifully, not all shower cakes require you to chant "not the momma, NOT the momma" under your breath while slicing into them. Some, for example, merely make you question what species of baby is being welcomed into the world:

Welcome Baby Tristan

While others offer almost refreshing inscription snafus:

Woohoo! It is time to par-tay, y'all, 'cuz *it a gril!*

This cake takes itself not only for the spelling and grammar errors, but for its cringe-inducing color choices and script execution. Bravo!

Also available in little-boy blue:

Here the decorator *did* remember the "s" (just barely), but then stumbled right at the finish line with that apostrophe placement:

Tiny footprints are a popular party theme, but some bakers seem to confuse footprints with actual *feet*. Others apparently think babies leave behind a layer of roasted skin with every wobbling step:

Our Family is growing by two feet

Baby Luke

Baby Luke, or Baby Howard?
(As in "the duck"? Yes? No?)

And here's the end-all be-all of baby-shower cakes:
the one, the only . . .

# naked mohawk-baby
## CARROT JOCKEYS

This cake is so disturbing, I'm almost glad the picture doesn't include the whole thing. The plastic clone babies wearing naught but mohawks are bad enough, but then they're also *riding carrots*. What do you do with that? It looks like some kind of perverted vegetable rodeo, or maybe a bizarre clone military exercise, what with their little plastic fists raised high in identical salutes.

I posted this cake on the blog just a month after Cake Wrecks began, and to this day it remains the standout favorite for many fans. Yep, these little carrot jockeys have accumulated quite the following, which I suppose will be useful when they make their move to take over the world. Wrecky world domination: That's the ticket.

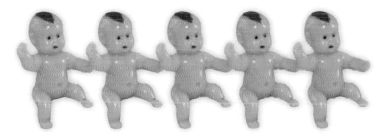

And what kind of occasion calls for a "naked babies riding carrots" decor, anyway? I mean, I'm going with baby shower to be on the safe side, but if I'm wrong I *really* don't want to know.

# Holiday Horrors

Too often what is billed as "the most wonderful time of the year" in actuality is the most depressing, stressful, "touch that last PlayStation game and so help me I will CUT you" time of the year. And I don't know about you, but when I'm on the verge of a particularly violent—albeit festive! homicide, I find that a well-placed baked good can help lure me off the warpath.

Fortunately, bakeries know this and have learned to treat our holiday icons with the appropriate amount of respect and care. Like this classic Christmas tree:

Which is apparently on wheels.

And what about every child's friend, Frosty?

"There must have been some magic in
That old ski cap they found.
For when they placed it on his head
He throttled everyone in town!"

And as for the kindly old elf himself, well, I don't think you parents need the threat of coal in the stocking anymore. Just tell your kids Santa is actually a raging psychopath intent on capturing and dismembering naughty children; these cakes can be your visual aids!

*"Look into my eyes . . . "*

"What are you lookin' at, punk? Huh? Why don't you take a picture; it'll last longer! What the—hey, put that camera down! Oooh, tough guy, eh? Yeah, okay, well, why don't you take my plastic cover off and stick your pinky in my mouth, then? Huh? HUH?"

"That's right, kids, after Santa dismembers the naughty children, he eats them. Now, whose turn was it to set the table? Oh, was it yours, Billy? Wonderful!"

x

This is Snappy, Santa's stitched-together Yuletide monster. He's made of sugar and spice and will mess your a$$ UP, beeyotches.

## Yule Love This

Alex writes,
"Last week was my coworker's last day, so I went to the local supermarket to get her a cake. I asked the bakery to write 'You will be missed' on it. The baker smartly replied 'That might not fit. Can I just write "You'll be missed?"'

"No problem; I figured this means she certainly understands the directions.

"I get the cake, and it reads YULE BE MISSED.

"As in . . . Christmas."

# When Gangsters Go "PC"
## FOR THE HOLIDAYS

"Bugsy, whaddaya doin'?"

"Just decoratin' this here Christmas cake, boss."

"Bugsy, you can't write 'Christmas' there—it's gonna offend somebody! An' don't call me 'boss.'"

"Sorry, boss. Can I write 'Happy Holidays'?"

"Nah, dat'll offend people who don't celebrate no holidays."

"Can I just use red and green icin' and not write nuthin'?"

"Bugsy, ya knucklehead, think about it: Red and green say 'Christmas,' see? S'no good. Use a lotta blue—but not blue and white, mind, 'cause dat's all Hanukkah-like. Maybe try blue and poiple."

"Yeah, but what do I *write*, boss?"

"I dunno; Li'l Antony said it's just gotta be 'completely nonoffensive-like, says nuthin' of substance, and don't reference no holidays.' Oh, and it can't start wit' 'happy' or 'merry,' neither—people might think we're forcing our 'emotional views' on 'em, whatever da heck *dat* means."

[sigh] "Okay, boss."

"Don't call me 'boss.'"

*(Turn the page to see Bugsy's completely inoffensive seasonal masterpiece!)*

Wow, I'm getting filled with the holiday spirit
just looking at this, aren't you? I think the underline
is what really sells it.

At first the characters
here were plain ol'
bakery employees,
but that was kind of
dull. I was trying to
figure out how to liven
things up when my
husband, John (who
is a wiz with accents),
suggested the gangster
twist. Obviously, the
idea of tough-talking
gangsters arguing
over how to decorate
a cake was simply
too absurd to pass up.
Plus, it allowed me
to work in a subtle
homage to one of
my favorite movies.
(What, you haven't
seen *Oscar*? Ah, you
haven't *lived* 'til
you've seen Tim Curry
giving Sly Stallone
"elocution lessons.")

Yes, Let's!

Baffling inscription?
Check.
Atmospheric pollution?
Check.
"Rotisserie chicken" label?
Check.
Excess punctuation?
Check, check, check, and check check.

# Random Wreckage

# Career Advice,
## CAKE WRECKS-STYLE

Lots of folks are looking for work these days, and judging by the number of people I see dancing on the side of the road holding Blimpie signs, I can only assume the pickin's are mighty slim.

So in the interest of bettering my fellow man (and woman), allow me to offer some time-tested,* expert-approved** advice when it comes to submitting your résumé:

## Put it on a cake.

You know, like this guy:

* Well, it worked for this guy; he got the job. That's one!
** I'm an expert on seeking approval, and I do approve. Unless you don't, that is, in which case it totally sucks.

Note how he resisted the temptation to write "Hire Me or Eat Me" and instead went with a far safer (yet barely legible) "Happy St. Patrick's Day." Oh, and that other bit? Well, the name of the company was "Safari Drive," so submitter Sara guesses he was going for "Safari Driven," which makes about as much sense as "Ga Fari Driver." Still, petty things like "meaning" pale drastically in comparison with that one phrase that makes every potential employer sit up and take notice: "Cake in the break room!"

Don't look at this cake as just a Wreck: Look at it as an inspiring example of single-minded tenacity.

Look how that inscription flows right down the side of the cake. That, my friends, is *commitment*! No namby-pamby dashes, squished text, or downward spirals here, no sir! This baker did not deviate, did not falter! S/he trudged onward even in the face of crippling ridicule, turning a deaf ear to naysayers, a blind eye to the warning signs of impending disaster, a numb hand to the piping bag, a stuffed-up nose to the smell of burning batter, and an insensate tongue to the bitter dregs of defeat!

[sits back down]

Okay, so maybe I was reaching a little with that metaphor. I thought I was doing pretty well until the "burning batter" bit, though. [taps teeth with pen] Huh.

# CAKE CAMOUFLAGE

As a Wreckerator, if you know you can't inscribe a legible greeting in icing to save your life, then you have but one option available to you: Hide it.

Good, *good*! Now no one will ever notice; it'd be like trying to pick out a polar bear in a snowstorm. Or a pile of crap in a mud heap. (You just pick the analogy that works for you, eh?)

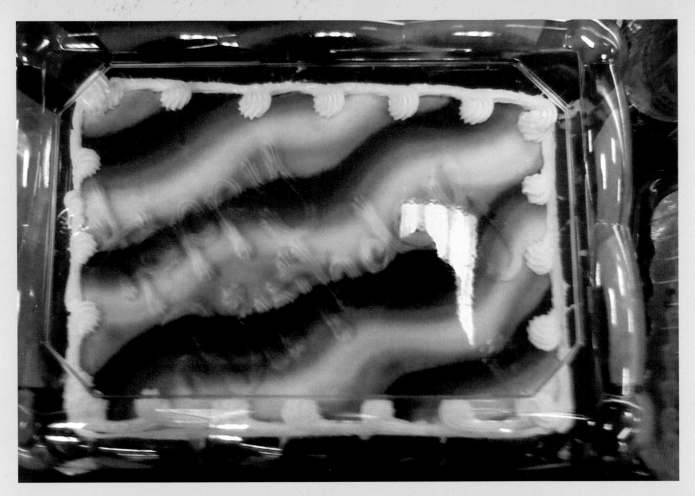

*Listen!* Do you smell that? I think I'm getting something from "the other side" . . .
[closing eyes] Yes . . . yes. Something is *definitely* trying to make contact here.

Dang, Winnie looks *piiissed*. But then I guess I would be, too, if MY leg were snapped off and reattached at the ankle. It also looks like he's making the swiping motion across the neck, in the universal "you are so dead" sign. Again, can you blame him?

[yelling] "Vortex of Doom! Get your Puce Swirling Vortex of Doom right here! Only $14.99! Great for parties! Vortex of Doom! Get your . . . "

In the murky realms between a cupcake and a CCC lies the disturbing little creation sometimes known as a "cupcake critter." This mini-monstrosity usually consists of two or three cupcakes completely encased in frosting—and yes, *many still have their paper wrappers on*. This leaves one with the unenviable dilemma of either fishing the wrapper out from under the piles of gooey frosting, or simply resigning oneself to ingesting a little extra fiber for the day.

**Cupcake critters range from the cute:**

"I utterly love you"? How moo-ving.

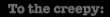

To the cringe-inducingly catastrophic:

*"Glug blurb gloppity gloo."*

"I WILL EAT YOUR SOUL."

Most cupcake critters are dogs. Interestingly enough, many cupcake critters are supposed to *look* like dogs, too.

Since making these dogs out of brown icing makes them look more like doggy by-products than dogs themselves (see "The Poo Phenomenon"), bakers usually make them out of a variety of Day Glo colors, which gives the consumer the *added* benefit of Technicolor poo.

## Cupcake critters: Poo the rainbow!

Of *course* it's a dog. He simply caught his head in a mechanical . . . rice picker. You know, as a child.

"Why, hello there! May I remind you that somewhere beneath my luscious cobalt exterior there may or may not be two paper cupcake wrappers? Yessiree. You have fun now, y'hear?"

## Tales from the Front:
## A Wreckporter Gets Ejected from the Premises.

Emily writes,

"Jen, I hope you're proud; I risked my Wii Fit for you!

"I was shopping with my two kids and had the impossible-to-find Wii Fit in my cart. I was looking for rolls, not even *considering* wreck-hunting, when bam: I was hit with three.

"They were all together, mocking me. I couldn't help it; I *had* to pull out my cell phone. There were four (four!?!) bakers behind the counter at this point, so I was trying to be sneaky. Well, I had almost snapped the last picture when a manager came sauntering over and asked me to kindly *go buy my Wii Fit* and leave. So, I snapped my last pic, said 'Sure!' and speed-walked to the nearest checkout.

(I didn't get my rolls.)

"Then as we were hurrying off, my son said, 'Mom, are we going to get the ugly green thing?' to which the manager glared and I laughed heartily. 'No, son,' I answered, 'we're getting kicked out of the store!'"

# Cake Wrecks:
## THE NEXT GENERATION

Here a few Wreckporters-in-Training (or WITs, for short) are mastering the art of the Nonverbal Wreck Reaction. Until they acquire a vocabulary capable of expressing their true feelings, these keen WITs will be forced to rely on one of the "Four Ds."

## NONVERBAL WRECK REACTION #1:
## DISGUST

Violet here is clearly appalled by her big sister Ruby's Pack O' Princesses cake, and as you can see, her nonverbal tirade speaks volumes.

Here's a rough translation: "Oh, how *original*! A pastel-prolific pack of princesses! Obviously my sister has succumbed to the brainwashing efforts of the blatant overcommercialization running rampant in our society. And just look at those gloppy roses and airbrushing—it's disgusting! Outrageous!

"Well, I suppose I *could* have a *little* piece. You know, just to be polite . . ."

# NONVERBAL WRECK REACTION #2:
# DESPAIR

Ryan here was *supposed* to get a super-spiffy Superman cake for his birthday party at the mall. Instead, the bakery made a purple-flowered tragedy with red swirly bits so amazingly UNspiffy that all of his friends had to flee the scene lest their coolness quotient drop precipitously from mere proximity. ("It had cooties.")

And so Ryan sits alone, poignantly communicating his feelings of deep disappointment in his family's utter *lack* of Superman-cake-acquiring skills.

Excellent work, Ryan! Good range, and that's an effective use of the "wistful side gaze" if I ever saw one.

# NONVERBAL WRECK REACTION #3:
# DESPONDEN

Some Wreckage is so bafflingly bad that it can send an unprepared viewer into a comalike state. Here little Caleb stares blankly at his Cupcake Cake, his young mind struggling to grasp how a baker could inflict such Wreckage upon an innocent like himself.

# NONVERBAL WRECK REACTION #4:
# DISBELIEF

Daniel may lack the words to express his outrage, but it's not hard to read this expression:

"Are you frickin' *kidding me*?!? I ask for a fire-truck cake, and you get me *this*?"

"It's melting—is it supposed to be melting? Is this some kind of character-building irony thing? 'Cuz I'm four now, and I am *totally* not falling for that anymore!"

Daniel stuck to his guns, too; he spent the next *year* telling anyone who would listen about his "broke-ed" fire-truck cake. Ah, I think I sense a kindred spirit here! Soon, Daniel-san, I shall introduce you to the wonders of "the Internet," groom your griping skills, instill you with a fondness for puns, and set you on the path of sarcasm and mockery for fun and profit! *Mwahahahaha!*

Oh, and that reminds me . . .

# come to the dark side;
## WE HAVE CAKE

For Erica's bridal shower her mom ordered a simple sheet cake, which, for reasons unknown, the bakery then decorated with a gigantic Darth Vader. The incident became so infamous in family lore that when the time came for Erica's baby shower, her mother knew *just* what to order.

Now, this is not a Wreck— oh no. This beauty made its debut on my "Sunday Sweets" feature online, and I do believe this could be the most awesome baby shower cake *ever*.

What, you doubt me? Then how about I count the ways this cake kicks every other baby shower cake's butt, eh?

1. Darth friggin' Vader is holding an adorable little beribboned baby girl on it. Really, we could just stop there. (But don't worry; we won't.)

2. Airbrushing that's actually . . . pretty? [gasp] Wait, you mean that's actually *possible*?!?

3. Best. Use of sprinkles. Ever. Baby want sprinkles? Baby gets sprinkles!

4. The lettering! The outline! The ruffly border! The *itty-bitty baby bottle*!!!

   [pauses to catch breath]

5. Say, did I mention that Darth Vader is holding a baby on it?

Case closed. Maximum awesomeness has been reached.

(Well, until someone makes a cake with *Spock* holding a baby girl, that is. Heheheh. Aw yeah.)

Hey, you made it through the whole book!